HILDA
BOSWELL'S

Treasury of Nursery Rhymes

COLLINS
PICTURE LIONS

Which is the way to London Town?

Which is the way to London Town?
To see the King in his golden crown.
One foot up and one foot down,
That's the way to London Town.

Which is the way to London Town?
To see the Queen in her silken gown.
Left, right, up and down,
Soon you'll be in London Town.

Simple Simon

Simple Simon met a pie-man
  Going to the fair;
Said Simple Simon to the pie-man:
  " Let me taste your ware."
Said the pie-man to Simple Simon:
  " Show me first your penny."
Said Simple Simon to the pie-man:
  " Sir, I haven't any."

A farmer went trotting

A farmer went trotting upon his grey mare,
Bumpety, bumpety, bump!
With his daughter behind him so rosy and fair,
Lumpety, lumpety, lump!

A raven cried "Croak!"
And they all tumbled down,
Bumpety, bumpety, bump!
The mare broke her knees,
And the farmer his crown,
Lumpety, lumpety, lump!

The mischievous raven,
Flew laughing away,
Bumpety, bumpety, bump!
And vowed he would serve them,
The same the next day,
Lumpety, lumpety, lump!

I'll sing you a song

I'll sing you a song,
Though not very long,
Yet I think it as pretty as any.
Put your hand in your purse,
You'll never be worse,
And give the poor singer a penny.

The lion and the unicorn

The lion and the unicorn,
Were fighting for the crown;
The lion beat the unicorn,
All round about the town.
Some gave them white bread
And some gave them brown;
Some gave them plum cake,
And sent them out of town.

Hickety, pickety, my black hen

Hickety, pickety, my black hen,
She lays eggs for gentlemen;
Gentlemen come every day,
To see what my black hen doth lay.

The swing

How do you like to go up in a swing,
Up in the air so blue?
Oh, I do think it the pleasantest thing
Ever a child can do!

Up in the air and over the wall,
Till I can see so wide,
Rivers and trees and cattle and all
Over the countryside—

Till I look down on the garden green,
Down on the roof so brown—
Up in the air I go flying again,
Up in the air and down!

Old Mother Hubbard

Old Mother Hubbard
Went to the cupboard,
    To get her poor Dog a bone;
But when she got there
The cupboard was bare,
And so the poor Dog had none.

    She went to the baker's
      To buy him some bread;
    But when she came back
      The poor Dog was dead.

    She went to the joiner's
      To buy him a coffin;
    But when she came back,
      The poor Dog was laughing.

    She took a clean dish
      To get him some tripe;
    But when she came back,
      He was smoking a pipe.

She went to the alehouse
  To get him some beer;
But when she came back,
  The Dog sat in a chair.

She went to the tavern
  For white wine and red;
But when she came back,
  The Dog stood on his head.

She went to the hatter's
  To buy him a hat;
But when she came back,
  He was feeding the cat.

The Dame made a curtsey,
  The Dog made a bow;
The Dame said,
    "Your servant."
The Dog said,
    "Bow-wow!"

Hark, hark, the dogs do bark

Hark, hark, the dogs do bark,
    The beggars are coming to town;
Some in rags, some in jags,
    And some in velvet gown.

Mary, Mary, quite contrary

Mary, Mary, quite contrary,
  How does your garden grow?
With silver bells and cockle shells,
  And pretty maids all in a row.

Humpty Dumpty

Humpty Dumpty sat on a wall,
Humpty Dumpty had a great fall;
All the King's horses and all the King's men
Couldn't put Humpty Dumpty
together again.

This little pig

This little pig went to market,

This little pig stayed at home,

Polly put the Kettle on

Polly, put the kettle on,
Polly, put the kettle on,
Polly, put the kettle on,
We'll all
have
tea.

Sukey, take it off again,
Sukey, take it off again,
Sukey, take it off again,
They've all
gone
away.

Sing a song of sixpence

Sing a song of sixpence,
    A pocket full of rye;
Four-and-twenty blackbirds
    Baked in a pie.
When the pie was opened,
    The birds began to sing;
Wasn't that a dainty dish
    To set before the King?

The King was in the Counting-house,
    Counting out his money;
The Queen was in the parlour,
    Eating bread and honey.
The maid was in the garden,
    Hanging out the clothes;
When down came a blackbird,
    And pecked off her nose.

Here we go round the mulberry bush

Here we go round
  the mulberry bush,
The mulberry bush,
  the mulberry bush;
Here we go round
  the mulberry bush,
On a cold
  and frosty
    morning.

This is the way we wash our hands,
Wash our hands,
   wash our hands;
This is the way we wash our hands,
On a cold
   and frosty
     morning.

This is the way we wash our clothes,
Wash our clothes,
   wash our clothes;
This is the way we wash our clothes,
On a cold
   and frosty
     morning.

I Had a Little Hen

I had a little hen,
   the prettiest ever seen,
She washed me the dishes
   and kept the house clean;
She went to the mill
   to fetch me some flour,
She brought it home
   in less than an hour.
She baked me my bread,
   she brewed me my ale;
She sat by the fire
   and told many
            a fine
               tale.

There was an old woman

There was an old woman tossed up in a basket,
Ninety times as high as the moon.
And where she was going I couldn't but ask it,
For in her hand she carried a broom.

"Old woman, old woman, old woman," quoth I.
"Oh whither, Oh whither, Oh whither, so high?"
"To sweep the cobwebs off the sky."
"Shall I go with you?" "Ay, by and by."

Boys and girls

come out to play

Boys and girls come out to play,
The moon doth shine as bright as day.
Leave your supper and leave your sleep,
And join your playfellows in the street.
Come with a whoop and come with a call,
Come with a good will or not at all.
Up the ladder and down the wall,
A half-penny loaf will serve us all;
You find milk, and I'll find flour,
And we'll have a pudding in half an hour.

Tom he was a piper's son

Tom he was a piper's son,
He learned to play when he was young,
But the only tune that he could play,
Was "Over the Hills and
        Far Away."

Now Tom with his pipe
   did play with such skill,
That those who heard him
   could never keep still,
Whenever they heard him
   they started to dance,
Even pigs on their hind legs
   would after him prance.

Goosey, goosey, gander

Goosey, goosey gander,
   Where shall I wander?
Upstairs, downstairs,
   In my lady's chamber.
There I met an old man
   Who wouldn't say his prayers,
I took him by his left leg,
   And threw him down the stairs.

Bobbie Shaftoe

Bobbie Shaftoe's gone to sea,
Silver buckles at his knee;
When he comes back, he'll marry me,
Bonny Bobbie Shaftoe!

Bobbie Shaftoe's bright and fair,
Combing down his yellow hair,
He's my ain for evermair,
Bonny Bobbie Shaftoe.

Cock Robin

Who killed Cock Robin?
I, said the Sparrow,
With my bow and arrow,
I killed Cock Robin.

Who saw him die?
I, said the Fly,
With my little eye,
I saw him die.

Who'll dig his grave?
I, said the Owl,
With my little trowel,
I'll dig his grave.

Who'll be the parson?
I, said the Rook,
With my little book,
I'll be the parson.

Who'll toll the bell?
I, said the Bull,
Because I can pull,
I'll toll the bell.

All the birds of the air
Fell a-sighing and a-sobbing
When they heard of the death
Of poor Cock Robin.

Twinkle, twinkle, little star

Twinkle, twinkle, little star,
How I wonder what you are,
Up above the world so high,
Like a diamond in the sky.

In the dark blue sky you keep,
Often through my curtains peep,
For you never shut your eye.
Till the sun is in the sky.

When the blazing sun is gone.
When he nothing shines upon,
Then you show your little light,
Twinkle, twinkle, all the night.

Then the traveller in the dark
Thanks you for your tiny spark;
How could he see where to go,
If you did not twinkle so.